曾經我眼

我擁有

To: Su
To share my love
in the Ancient Art of
China with you!

Vic H 3/01

Once I owned this collection;
now it exists in my mind's eye.

A green jade pendant my parents gave to me when I was four years old first whetted my appetite for collecting things. Like other children, I began to hoard bus tickets, matches, and cigarette boxes, and by the time I was ten years old, I had developed an excellent stamp collection.

From those beginnings, I turned to collecting seals, ink stones, and paintings, bamboo carvings and snuff bottles, bronze buddhas, porcelain, and other types of Chinese art.

In the late 70's, I was presented with a golden opportunity to expand my collections. China had been in the throes of the Cultural Revolution (1966-1976); many antiques and works of art had been destroyed, but a lot had also been sold to the government at very low prices. At the time, the Chinese government did not have an antique bureau, and these artifacts were handled by the import/export bureau. Works of art could be purchased from antique stores in all the major cities and exported legally. After the Cultural Revolution, an antique bureau was eventually set up.

During the late 70's and 80's, I traveled from city to city and from province to province; from Hebei, Shanxi and Shandong in the north, south through Hangzhou and Guangzhou, and westwards into Sichuan; and of course, I frequented the major cities such as Beijing, Tianjin, and Shanghai. Scholar's items could be found in

p.2 **Earthenware Jar with Mineral Pigments, Machang Phase of Gansu** Neolithic BC 4800~2800 37cm(H)
Oxford TL test no.: PH993/222

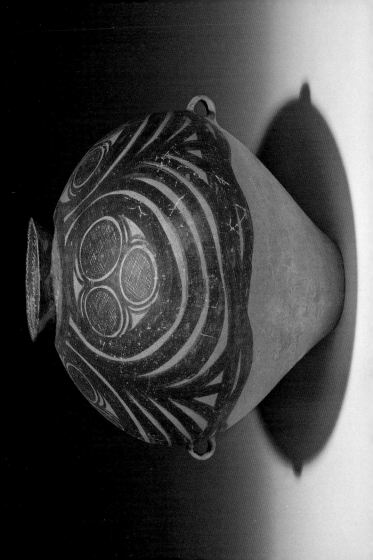

the Jiannan region, the cities of Shouzhou, Wuseck, Jiangsu, Zheungzhou, Nianjing, and Yeungzhou.

I did not buy according to a budget at the time. I just felt that I should acquire and conserve as much material as possible. Later, I had to sell some things in order to support further purchases. It was during this period that the idea arose of sharing with others my passion for collecting.

By integrating my career with my love of Chinese culture, I am fulfilling my dream of sharing this culture with others. Many people ask why I chose to name my galleries "DRAGON CULTURE". This name is an expression of my aspiration to preserve and contribute to the culture of the Dragon that is China. One of the great pleasures of my life has been the opportunity to meet with people from all over the world who share my love of Chinese (Dragon) culture.

Today, in mainland China, many people do not have the aesthetic understanding to appreciate and preserve Chinese antiques. Much of their heritage will be destroyed with the construction of the Chang Jiang Sanxia Dam. By looking after the Chinese antiques you acquire, you will be making a contribution to the protection and preservation of Chinese culture, one of the oldest cultures in the world. I believe that as the country develops and prospers,

p.4 Archaic Bronze Gu
   Shang BC 1600~1100   23cm(H)

the people of mainland China will begin collecting and conserving this nation's great cultural heritage. It will then become very expensive to collect Chinese antiques. Indeed, the first signs of this process are already apparent in some categories.

Like many other collectors, I came across a lot of questions such as "How to avoid buying fakes in the market? What determines the value and price of a piece? How do I start my collection? What should I collect from each dynasty?" I also experienced discouragement when I bought a fake piece. Many wonderful, indeed fantastic works of art can be seen in galleries along Hollywood Road, named one of the top ten shopping streets in the world. However there are also many reproductions in the market. I designed this short primer to give beginners some basic concepts and the knowledge necessary for making the most of their collection.

Through our web site: www.dragonculture.com.hk, there are 4 main areas you can explore:

1. *Ignite your sense of art*
We will show you a vast selection of pieces from various dynasties, and let you appreciate them, really "see" them without the distraction of descriptive text. We will let you discover yourself what is really beautiful, noble, unusual...

2. *We bring you not only authentic Chinese antiques, but also history and culture*

p.6 Bronze Tripod (Ding)
   Western Zhow BC 1027~771   21cm(H)

By working with scholars to provide you with interesting information regarding each work of art, its historical background and its meaning, we aim to give you the basic knowledge and the understanding necessary for you to make the most of your collection, and further your enjoyment.

3. *Your Chinese antique consultant*

Giving you professional advice and guiding you in the right direction in collecting Chinese antiques.

4. *Available items*

This section presents authentic Chinese antiques available at wholesale or retail with our unique "triple sales guarantee".

I aim to communicate to you the joy and excitement of the rich heritage of Chinese (Dragon) culture through this primer, my collection (*Once I owned this collection; now it exists in my mind's eye.*) and the web site. I hope that it will contribute to the understanding and appreciation of Chinese culture at every level throughout the world. The information from this primer and the website will eliminate unnecessary costs in order to allow you to acquire more pieces within the same budget. Collecting Chinese art should not be the privilege of the rich. I hope that your interest and appreciation will impart a new life to Chinese art and culture.

Victor Choi

p.8 **Bronze Bell**
   Spring and Autumn BC 771~475   25cm(H)

I want to thank Professor *Donald T. Critchlow*
and *Arthur Hwang* for helping me write this book,
Cindy Au Yeung and *Ada Yung* for assisting on its production.
The photographs were taken by my dear friend *C. L. Chow*,
a professional photographer who has worked for
many years for Sotheby's.

p.10 **Bronze Ding with Cover**
  Warring States BC 206~221   23cm(H)

MOST OFTEN ASKED QUESTIONS

1. How do I start my collection?   15
2. How can I avoid buying a fake in the market?   19
3. What determines the value and price of a piece and   23
   how can I get the best bargains in Hong Kong?
4. Is it legal to take an antique out of Hong Kong?   31
5. Can I ship the piece home without it being broken?   33
6. What should I collect from each dynasty?   45

p.12 **Painted Grey Earthenware Figure**
Western Han BC 206~AD 8   52cm(H)
Oxford TL test no.: c299673

11
~

REPRESENTATIVE ILLUSTRATIONS

Neolithic	B.C.8000-2100	59
Shang	B.C.1600-1027	71
Zhou - Western Zhou	B.C.1027-771	79
- Eastern Zhou	B.C.770-221	
- Spring & Autumn	B.C.770-471	
- Warring States	B.C.475-221	
Han	B.C.206-AD 220	107
Three Kingdoms	A.D.420-589	163
Jin	A.D.265-420	167
Northern & Southern Dynasties	A.D. 420-589	175
- Northern Wei	A.D. 386-535	
- Northern Chi	A.D. 550-577	
Sui	A.D. 581-618	193
Tang	A.D. 618-907	199
Song	A.D. 960-1279	241
Yuan	A.D. 1271-1368	257
Ming	A.D. 1368-1644	267
Qing	A.D. 1644-1911	281
Early 20th Century		303

p.14 **Three Painted Grey Earthenware Figures**
Western Han BC 206~AD 8   60cm(H)
Oxford TL test no.: c299h9, c299h10, c299q87

1. How do I start my collection?

$\mathcal{F}$irst, choose a piece that you like, as it will be in your collection for a long while.

You need to decide what kind of piece you would like. Which dynasty do you like? Do you want a vase, a figure, an animal, or a stone carving? How much do you want to spend on? In Hollywood Road, you can start your budget from US$100 to what you can afford.

A Han piece might be simpler in style, while a Tang or Ming piece might be more sophisticated in detail and glazing. Still, each piece varies in quality within a dynasty. The beauty and workmanship of a piece should bring you happiness. A reputable antique consultant can give you advice on the workmanship of a piece, as well as guide you according to your own aesthetic tastes and budget.

If you are still not certain as to what you want, we recommend reading a catalogue of a major auction house such as Sotheby's or Christie's or a good book on Chinese art.

Second, the piece must be authentic. The reputation of the dealer is important. Ask if the gallery provides a certificate from Oxford Authentication Ltd., which is used by Christie's and Sotheby's. This certificate will enhance the resale value of your piece. We want to emphasize that the dealer should be willing to bear the

p.16 **Five Painted Grey Earthenware Soldiers**
Western Han BC 206~AD 8   48 cm(H)

costs of testing if the Oxford test is negative. (Refer to the following section on authenticity.)

The third criterion is quality. Quality is the key to the purchase of any antique. In Hong Kong today, one can see and purchase the highest quality of Chinese antiquities anywhere in the world.

A reputable antique consultant should be ready to tell you if the piece has been restored and point out where this restoration has taken place. Also, the dealer should be willing to compare the quality of pieces that have appeared recently in major auction house catalogues. Origins, condition, workmanship, detail, and the uniqueness of the piece will determine quality.

p.18 **Rare Sichuan Pottery Figure of a Buddha**
Eastern Han AD 23~AD 220   20cm(H)

2. How can I avoid buying a fake in the market?

This is a simple question, but a may have complex answer depending on the piece you purchase. For wooden pieces there are universities such as the University of Toronto and laboratories to provide Carbon 14 testing. Bronzes can be authenticated at London University. For jade, stone, and glass there are different techniques to determine authenticity.

For pottery pieces, Oxford University provided an authenticity certificate based on the Thermoluminescence Test. This test is quite accurate for dating to within a few hundred years of the creation of a piece. Doreen Stoneham, a well-known expert in Chinese antiquities based in London, provides this test through the company she founded, Oxford Authentication, Ltd. She has more than 28 years experience and has surveyed more than 30,000 pieces. Her assistant Phyllis Hsia takes samples from pieces in Hong Kong and sends them directly to London for testing. Sotheby's and Christie's auction houses use her reports.

While this test certifies authenticity, a professional dealer still assesses each piece according to its patina, style, weight, color, hardness of clay and general look.

Actually, the spirit, the soul of a piece is the key to

p.20 **Large Sichuan Pottery Figure of a Witch Doctor**
Eastern Han AD 23~AD 220   100cm(H)
Oxford TL test no.: c299h14

indentifying whether it is authentic or not. The form and colour can easily be imitated, but what cannot be imitated is the soul, that is, the essence of a Chinese antique.

This ability to "eye" a piece in evaluating its authenticity and value can only be acquired through experience that comes from looking at hundreds of pieces. In order to ignite your sense of art and to achieve a better understanding of the history and culture behind each work, you should see and touch authentic pieces by visiting museums and galleries, and delve into the relevent literature.

The antique consultant is very important as he guides you in the right direction, provides you with information on the history and culture behind each work of art and may allow you to avoid paying the extra expense of an Oxford test. Always find a dealer who is knowledgeable, professional, has an established reputation and has been in business for a long time. Still, if you are in doubt about a piece, ask the dealers if their galleries provide Oxford certification and whether they will bear the cost of the test if the results are negative.

p.22 **Amber and Green Glazed Pottery Incense Burner and Lamp Stand** Han BC 206~AD 220   23cm, 18cm(H)

3. What determines the value and price of a piece and how can I get the best bargain in Hong Kong?

The value of a piece is determined by aesthetic beauty, workmanship, condition, supply and demand. Pieces made for an emperor usually reflect the highest quality of workmanship, while pieces made for imperial officials and wealthy merchants will have less value. Yet, even this can vary depending on the time the piece was produced. Some items produced for one emperor might be less valuable than pieces produced for another emperor; something made for a great noble might be more valuable than a piece made for a weak king. Thus the historical background of the piece plays an important role in its valuation.

Aesthetic attraction, craftsmanship and uniqueness will be reflected in the price of an item. Nonetheless, prices vary considerably over time, depending on supply and demand. For example, new discoveries of a Han tomb will add to the supply of artifacts from this period, thereby reducing the price of items from this dynasty; figures of officers have more value than those of soldiers as they are more rare.

Demand also determines prices. Obviously, if more people want pieces from a certain period, this demand will drive up prices.

p.24 **Amber-Glazed Red Pottery Figure of a Dog**
Eastern Han AD23-220 23cm (H)
Oxford TL Test no. c200f86

Art from the Tang dynasty might be more in demand than art from the Han period. The same rule applies within a dynasty. Collectors will consider pieces produced in the reign of one emperor more valuable than items produced in the reign of another emperor, depending on the historical importance of the emperor. Even with a specific reign certain items will be considered more valuable. Thus the demand for Tang "Fat" lady figures might be more than that for an equivalent Tang male figure, thereby raising the price.

Sometimes, collectors or antique dealers interested in certain kinds of pieces also jack up the price. The prices of tomb pieces can be higher than those of works from the Ming and Ching imperial period and marked ceramics from 50 years ago.

Furthermore, where you buy the piece affects the price. Hong Kong is the only city in China you can buy and ship Chinese antique to your country legally. British law still applies because of the "one country two systems" policy. All kinds of Chinese antiques are shipped to Hollywood Road in Hong Kong for resale. Thus Hollywood Road was elected as one of the top ten shopping streets in the world. Tourists, dealers, collectors and museum curators from the US, Europe and other countries come here to do their sourcing everyday. Overseas collectors bear the cost of dealers' travelling expenses, salaries, shipping costs, insurance, advertising, consult-

p.26 **Green-Glazed Pottery Duck Pool**
   Han BC 206~AD 220   24cm(L)

ant commissions, etc. As a consequence there is generally a price difference between 3 to 7 times of what you would pay if you buy directly in Hong Kong, where most shops work with low profit margins in order to achieve high turnover. However, a considerable number of shops in Hong Kong will try to sell you reproductions as genuine antiques, so you need to work with a reputable and established dealer (refer to Question 2 about authenticity).

Also, auctions in the United States and Europe tend to raise the market value of Chinese antiques in the West. Although many people prefer using an auction house, auctions tend to be much more expensive than purchasing directly from a Hong Kong dealer. Auction houses set higher prices in order to cover their promotion and auction fees. Therefore, you should not be surprised to find better quality pieces at lower prices in Hong Kong than you will find in most American or European auctions.

Nowadays, you can purchase authentic Chinese antiques in Hong Kong at surprisingly low prices that can be less than what one would pay for a modern art piece. For example, a genuine Neolithic painted pot over three thousand years old or a Han horse (BC 206-AD 200) or Tang figure (AD 618-907) can be purchased for only a couple hundred dollars (US). Of course, more exquisite and rare pieces can cost considerably more, but even these pieces can be ba-

p.28 **Green-Glazed Pottery Watch Tower**
    Han BC 206~AD 220   40cm(H)

rgains, given their age, workmanship, and aesthetic beauty.

Remember that in the end, the ultimate value of a piece is determined by you. Not everyone likes the same thing. This is what makes building a collection fun.

p.30 **Green-Glazed Pottery Bowl with Handle**
   Han BC 206~AD 220   21cm(H)

4. Is it legal to take an antique out of Hong Kong?

The "One Country, Two Systems" and the "50 years un-changed promise" made by the People's Republic of China to the Hong Kong people allows you to take authentic Chinese antiques out of Hong Kong, legally and tax free.

It is illegal to ship any antique more than 50 years old out of mainland China. Thus Hong Kong is the only city in China where you can purchase an artifact more than fifty years of age and ship it home legally.

Remember to get an official receipt from the gallery that states the period of the piece, the cost, and when it was purchased in Hong Kong.

p.32 **Green-Glazed Pottery Figures of a Ram and a Chicken**
Han BC 206-AD 220   15cm(L), 12cm(L)

5. Can I ship the piece home without it being broken?

There are 5 ways to ship your purchases. The volume weight, size and fragility, would determine your choice. (please see attachment for shipping rate and details)

1. Federal Express

- It is the most cost-effective way for various antique items
- Although the maximum insurance coverage of FedEx is USD 500, we find that they never lose the items as they have a very good computer tracking system to locate the parcel.
- Although some shipping agents can arrange full insurance, the total shipping cost may be doubled. Furthermore, when the pieces are broken, you have to go through a series of procedures to lodge a claim. Generally, many credit cards such as American Express provide you the damage insurance. Please check with your bank whether you are entitled to such a policy.
- Clients will bear any taxes or duties related to the import of items to their country.

p.34 **Green-Glazed Pottery Watch Tower with Figures**
Eastern Han AD 23-220   95cm(H)

- **_Calculation by volume weight:_**

  In order to make the piece arrive safely, please add 5 inches to each side for packing. The more inches you add the more expensive it is, but of course, the safer it is.

  For example:
  - *Size of item: 5" x 10" x 5"*
  - *Estimated size after packing: 15" x 20" x 15"*
  - *Volume Weight: (15 x 20 x 15) / 366 = 12.3kg*

- **Wooden Box:**

  Taking safety into consideration, packing into a wooden box is recommended. It costs from HKD 300 ~ HKD 600 each depending on the size.

2. Via a professional shipping agent by air

- For expensive or fragile items, you can use a professional shipping agent to ship it door-to-door with *full insurance*. Michelle Int'l Transport, Jardine, Sun Ming Transportation are the major shippers on this type.

- But, you must use their professional packing

- The shipping cost may be around 2 times or even more than using Federal Express.

p.36 **Grey Pottery Figure of a Horse**
Nothern Wei AD 386-535   28cm(H)
Oxford TL Test no: PH993/146 C199U3

- *Michelle International Transportation Co. Ltd.*
  Tel: 852-2897-1080   Fax: 852-2897-1645
  e-mail: michelle@attglobal.net

- *Sun Ming Transportation Co. Ltd.*
  Tel: 852-2757-3868   Fax: 852-2757-3533
  e-mail: ngwillia@netvigator.com

- *Jardine International Movers Ltd.*
  Tel: 852-2563-6698   Fax: 852-2620-0354
  e-mail: liza.ng@jardine-logistics.com.hk

3. Via a shipping agent by Sea

- Many dealers choose to ship bulky, or inexpensive merchandise via a shipping agent by sea. Universal Transportation and Cargo Express are the major shippers of this type.
- Port-to-Port service is mostly the case
- Full insurance / loss insurance is provided
- Generally, free packing is provided by the gallery
- A Wooden Box is a must

p.38 **Painted Buff Pottery Figure of a Caparisoned Horse**
Northern Wei Dynasty AD 386~535   37cm(H)
Oxford TL test no.: c198272

- *Universal Transportation Co. Ltd.*
  Tel: 852-2501-0930   Fax: 852-2523-0683
  e-mail: ajyiu@netvigator.com

- *Cargo Express International Ltd.*
  Tel: 2763-6667   Fax: 2342-8663
  e-mail: cargoexp@netvigator.com

4. Hand Carrying on Plane

- If you go home directly and the purchase is not big or fragile, or very expensive, hand carrying is recommended.
- This is the best and cheapest way to bring it home.
- Generally, the maximum size is 20" x 14' x 19", but you can always get a special arrangement from the airline especially if you are travelling business class or first class.

5. Post Office

- By air
  - It is only recommended for inexpensive and small items, as Federal Express, DHL, UPS provide a better service in term of cost and efficiency.

p.40 **Rare Painted Grey Pottery Figure of a Kneeling Bactrian Camel**   Late 6th Century/ Early Tang Dynasty   27.9cm(L)
Oxford TL test no.: 866j86

- By sea
  - This is very highly recommended for those bulky items, less than 16 kg in weight, not fragile and not urgently required as it is the cheapest way.

Insurance

Shipping agent

- Insurance premium depends on coverage, and vary among agents, you can buy full insurance including breakage, full insurance excluding breakage or loss only.
- Please noted that claims may be subjected to a policy which subtracts a certain percentage of the shipment value.

  For example:
  - *The shipment value is HKD 10000.*
  - *It is subject to policy excess of 10% of shipment value*
  - *In case of loss or damage the maximum amount of reimbursement would be HKD 9000 [HKD1000 (1-10%)]*

- For all risk insurance, the insured items have to be packed by the agents themselves
- Generally, full insurance will not cover the following:
  - Loss, damage or expense arising from pre-existing dam-

p.42 **Very Large and Rare Grey Pottery Figure of a Bactrian Camel**   Late 6th Century/Early Tangy Dynasty   80cm (H)
Oxford TL test no.: c298h59

age of the interest insured,even though such damage has been repaired or restored, partly or completely

- Loss of market, delay, loss of use, clean up costs

- In the event of damage to antiques items insured, liability may be restricted to reasonable cost of repairs and no claim is recoverable in respect of depreciation.
- Thus, the final compensation may be the restoration fee only. This depends on the survey reports, the conditions of the items etc.

Federal Express

- Limit of liability is USD 500 for antique items
- In case of loss or damage, notice should be made within 15 days from the date on which the shipment should have been delivered

All of the above information (provided by the shipping agents/ companies) is for reference only, and may subject to change according to the respective agent/company. Please contact the related agents directly for details and refer to the relevant certificate of insurance should you have any inquiries.

p.44 **Very Large and Rare Grey Pottery Figure of a Reclining Bactrian Camel** Late 6th Century/Early Tangy Dynasty 35cm(H)
Oxford TL test no.: c298h60

6. What should I collect from each dynasty?

The long history of China, one of the oldest in the world, has revolved around dynasties, the reign of imperial families. Some of these dynasties lasted hundreds of years, while some only a generation or two. "We not only bring you authentic Chinese antique, but also history and culture" in our web site provides a brief historical background to the dynastic culture. You will also have a better idea on what you can collect after you look at the representative illustrations from this primer.

Art produced in each dynasty is usually quite distinctive. It won't take long before you will be able to identify a Neolithic pot, a Han horse, a Tang "Fat" lady, or a Ming vase. One can learn a lot from the many excellent books on Chinese art; studying catalogues from the auction houses will also add to your knowledge. However, the best way to learn is to visit the museums and galleries in Hong Kong and to look at the pieces yourself.

p.46 **Painted Red Pottery Figure of a Camel**
    Tang Dynasty AD 618~907   35cm(H)
    Oxford TL test no.: c100b36

REFERENCE BOOKS

General

- Yu Weichao, **A Journey into China's Antiquity,** Morning Glory Publishers, 1997.

- Julia M. White, Ronald T. Otsuka, **Pathway to the Afterlife: Art from Sze Hong Collection,** Denver Art Museum & University of Hawaii Press, 1993.

- **States to the Han periods excavated in Hubei province,** Hubei Provincial Museum & The Art Gallery, The Chinese University of Hong Kong, 1994.

- professor Liu Liang-Yu, **Early Wares: Prehistoric to Tenth Century,** Aries Genmini Publishing Ltd, 1991.

Religious Sculptures

- Zoungxu, **Xian World - Acient Chinese Capital for over a Thousand Years,** Shaanxi People's Fine Arts Publishing House, 1990

p.48 **Painted Red Pottery Figure of a Camel and Rider**
Tang Dynasty AD 618~907   47 cm(H)
Oxford TL test no.: c99n15

- Chan Wai Ha, Li yuk Man, **The Art of Contemplation - Religious Sculpture from Private Collections,** National Palace Museum, 1997.

Stone Sculptures
- Wang Qian, **The Ancient Stone Sculptures in Shannxi Province,** Shannxi People's Art Publishing House Xian, 1985.

Snuff Bottles
- Cheung Lim Sun, **Snuff Bottles in the Collection of the National Palace Museum,** National Palace Museum, 1991.

Terra-cotta
- Li Rui Lin, **Emperor Qin Shihuang's Eternal Terra-cotta Warriors and Horses- A Mighty and Valiant Underground Army over 2,200 Years Back,** Shannxi Sanqin Publishing House, 1994.

p.50 **Painted Grey Pottery Figure of an Earth Spirit, Zhen Mu Shou** Late 6th Century/ Early Tang 35cm(H)
Oxford TL test no.: c298d22

- Patricia Berger, Jennifer Randolph Casler, **Tomb Treasures from China - The Buried Art of Acient Xian,** Kimbell Art Museum, Fort Worth, and the Asian Art Museum of San Francico, 1994.

- **Spirit of Han,** the Southeast Asian Ceramic Society & Sun Tree Publishing Ltd., 1991.

- Willian Lindesay, **The Terracotta Army of the First Emperorof China,** Odyssey Publications Ltd., 1998.Yuen Ware

- Lin Shwu-shin, Hsieh Ming-liang, Chang Wei-hwa, **Spe cial Exhibition of Early Chinese Greenware - Principally Yuen Ware,** Nien-His Foundation, 1996.

REFERENCE MAGAZINES
- **Arts of Asia,** Arts of Asia Publications Limited, Hong Kong. Web site: www.artsofasianet.com

- **Orientations,** Orientations Magazine Ltd., Hong Kong. Email: infro@orientations.com.hk

p.52 **Rare Painted Grey Pottery Figure of a Man**
  Late 6th Century/ Early Tang   90cm(H)

MUSEUMS OF CHINESE ART

China

- **Emperor Qin Shi Huang's Museum**
  Address: Xian, China

- **National Museum of Chinese History**
  Address: Beijing, China

- **Palace Museum**
  Address: Beijing, China

- **Shanghai Museum**
  Address: Shanghai, China

- **Shanxi History Museum**
  Address: Intersaction of Xiao Zhai East Road and Cui Hua
  Road, Xian, China

Hong Kong

- **Hong Kong Museum of Art**
  Web site: www. icsd.gov.hk/ce/museum/arts/index/html
  Address: 10 Salisbury Road, Tsim Sha Tsui, Kowloon, Hong Kong

p.54 **Rare Painted Red Pottery Figure of a Court Lady with
a Bird** Tang Dynasty AD 618~907 44cm(H)
Oxford TL test no.: 866f67

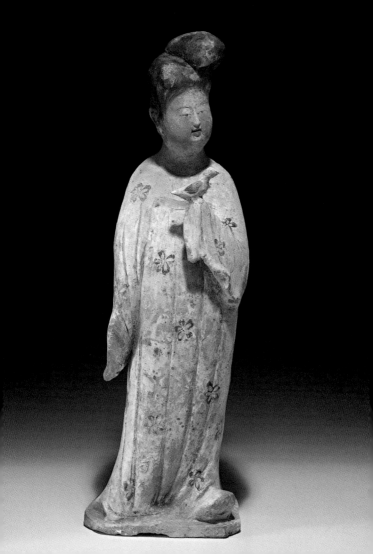

University Museum & Art Gallery, The University of Hong Kong
Web site: hkumag
Address: 94 Bonham Road, Hong Kong

Taiwan

National Palace Museum
Web site: www.npm.gov.tw
Address: Wai-shuang-his, Shih-lin, Taipei 11102, Taiwan

USA

Asian Art Museum of San Francisco
Web site: www.asianart.org
Address: Golden Gate Park, San Francisco, California, USA

Metropolitan Museum of Art, New York
Web site: www.metmuseum.org

Museum of Fine Arts, Boston
Web site: www.boston.com

p.56 **Rare Pair of Painted Red Pottery Figures of Court Ladies with Birds**   Tang Dynasty AD 618~907   34cm(H)
Oxford TL test no.: c866f48, c 866f49

Museum of Fine Arts San Francisco
Web site: www.famsf.org

UK

British Museum
Web site: www.british-museum.ac.uk
Address: Great Russell Street, London WC1B 3DG, UK

AUCTION HOUSES

Christie's
Web site: www.christies.com

Sotheby's
Web site: www.sothebys.com

p.58 **Rare and Large Pair of Painted Red Pottery Figures of a Fat Lady and a Man**   Tang Dynasty AD 618~907   50cm(H)
Oxford TL test no.: c199z42, c199x85

NEOLITHIC BC 8000-2100

*D*uring the Neolithic period, human groups in China established sedentary, agricultural villages and began making pottery. By the end of the Neolithic period, some groups were living in highly stratified societies ruled by powerful leaders. The Neolithic period ended with the introduction of Bronze vessels for use in rituals around 200BC. The area covered by what is now modern China was made up of distinct regions each with its own separate identity. Based on the similarities in such things as pottery, houses and style of burials, archaeologists have identified many different cultures.

Many Neolithic cultures flourished during the years 5000-3000 BC. The YangShao culture of the central plains of Shannxi Henan was well known for painted pottery. They were often decorated in black paint with complex design. After the YangShao Culture came, the LongShan culture which flourished in the lower Huang He. They produced extremely delicate eggshell-thin pottery.

The Majiayao, Banshan and Machang cultures developed in the upper Huang He and produced various types of pottery. In the Dawenkou culture of Shandong and North Jiangsu, pottery was more sophisticated. Vessels more frequently had appendages such as spouts legs and ring-bases. Their tombs were usually made of

p.60 **Earthenware Vessel with Mineral and Leaf Pigments, Gansu Yang Shao Culture, Banshan Phase**   40cm(H)

elaborately constructed chambers filled with objects of jade, ivory, turquoise and black/white-ware.

      The Hong Shan culture in Liaoning, Northern Hebei produced painted pottery and large amounts of jade carving. In the lower region of River Changjiang, the Liangzhu culture also produced jade carving. This culture is well known for its great variety of jade carving as well as superb carving techniques. The most important of these carvings are the ceremonial disks (bi), broad-bladed axes (yue) and ritual tubes (cong).

p.62 **Two Earthenware vessels with Mineral and Rain Pigments, Gansu Yang Shao Culture, Bansan Phase** 33cm, 37cm(H)

P.64 **Rare and Large Red Pottery Tripot Vessel, Gansu Yang Shao Culture** 45cm(H)
Oxford TL test no.: c100d61

p.65 **Red Pottery Ewer with Handle and Swallow Mouth, Gansu** 23cm(H)

p.66 **Rare Pair of White Pottery Kuei Vessel with Handles, Ta-Wen-K'ou Culture** 27cm(H)
Oxford TL test no.: c100b41

p.67 **Rare Thin Red Pottery Jar with Handle, Qi Jia Culture** 22cm(H)
Oxford TL test no.: c199x25

p.68 **Rare Red Pottery Jar with Handle and Four Mouths, Qi Jia Culture** 15cm(H)

p.69 **White Jade Axe Suffused with Greyish White** 16cm(L)

p.70 **Green Jade Axe and Green Jade Column Suffused with Greyish White** 8cm (L), 6.7cm(L)

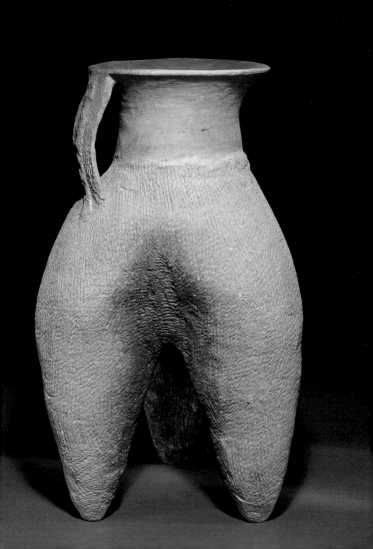

SHANG BC 1600-1100

$\mathcal{F}$rom 2000BC to 500BC, Chinese civilization blossomed with the development of a writing system, the discovery of advanced bronze metallurgy, and the beginning of urban centers, with palaces, temples, and the workshops of specialized industries. In this highly stratified society, hundreds of polities emerged, including three powerful dynastic states, Xia, Shang, Zhou. The Xia Culture was discovered through the archaeological finds in 1959 at Erlitou in Henan (South of the Yellow River). The unearthed bronze artifacts marked the beginning of the Bronze Age in Ancient China.

The most important ritual symbols of this age were bronze vessels. The manufacture of bronze vessels required abundant resources and intensive labor.

While the finest flowering of Shang art is seen in its bronzes, primitive greenware pottery appeared in the late Shang period. There has been considerable speculation as to how it originated. Archeological sites from the middle of the Shang period have been discovered in modern Honan, Hoph, and Shansi that show numerous examples of a hard pottery with impressed decoration, with a purplish-brown body. The high temperature porcelleanous glaze used at this time and during the late Shang period reveals the development of primitive porcelain. Still, much remains unknown about Shang culture.

p.72 **Grey Pottery Tsun Vessel** 18cm(H)

REPRESENTATIVE ILLUSTRATIONS

p.74 **Archaic Bronze Jue**   21cm(H)

p.75 **Archaic Bronze Ding**   25cm(H)

p.76 **Archaic Bronze Lui and Mao Spear**   3.8cm(H)

p.77 **White Jade Figure with Ram Head Decoration**   3.8cm(H)

p.78 **Jade Needle Suffused with White and A Yellow Jade Ornament (kau)**   7.2cm(H), 2.3cm(L)

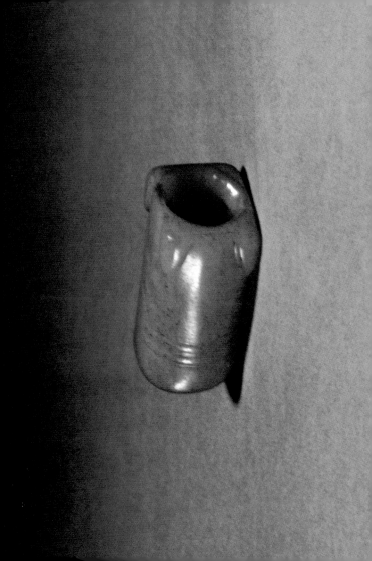

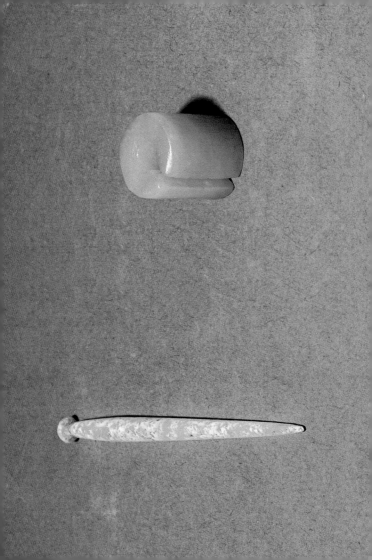

Zhou BC 1100-256
(Western Zhou BC 1027-771)
(Eastern Zhou BC 770-221)
Chunqui (Spring/Autumn) BC 770-471
Warring States BC 471-221

*I*n the year 1122 BC, a rebel tribal chieftan from the Zhou tribe defeated the last Shang emperor Ti-hsin Tzu-shou at the famous battle of Muyeh. The Shang army with 70,000 troops was completely routed by the 45,000 strong Zhou forces. The Shang emperor fled to his capitol and burned himself to death in the Deer Pavilion. After 662 years the Shang dynasty was no more.

Chi Fa established a new capital in modern Sian in 1121 B. C. He dropped the title of emperor and became King Wu. In 771 BC nomads forced the Zhou king to move the capitol eastwards to Loyang. This ended the western Zhou period and created the Eastern Zhou (B.C. 770-221).

Clearly influenced by Shang culture, Western Zhou pottery can be categorized as utilitarian, architectural, and primitive green ware. For the first time, primitive glazing occurs in pottery, an historic advance in pottery technique. This primitive glazing is found in Yueh pottery. A small number of pottery figurines have been found,

p.80 **Primitive Porcelain (Yueh Ware) Yellowish-Glazed Jar with Dragon Pattern**   Western Zhou BC 1027~771   21cm(H)

but such finds are extremely rare.

Only with the move to Loyang did a distinctive Eastern Zhou art culture emerge. Following the usage of Confucius, Chinese historians refer to the Eastern Zhou period as the Spring and Autumn period. Warfare during this time led to advances in philosophy, commerce and technology. Significant changes occurred in kiln structure that allowed for new firing techniques that provided more even glazing. Green ware emerges fully developed.

The Spring/Autumn period ended in BC475 with the defeat of the state of Lu by the Ch'u. The Warring States period followed, characterized by intense warfare between seven rival states. The Warring States period continued the techniques developed in the Spring/Autumn period. Green ware from the Kiangsu and Chekiang region is often elegant in design, with fine greenish-white clay and green glaze with a hint of blue. Besides green ware, ceramics are typified by gray painted ware and incised black ware. Ceramics were made to imitate bronzes. This kind of ware was produced by intense firing at temperatures over 1,000 degrees Celsius, and incised with a sharp steel knife.

p.82 **Archaic Bronze Gui**
Western Zhou BC 1027~771　21cm(H)

p.84 **Jade Figures of a Fish and an Animal Suffused with White**
Zhou BC 1027~221   10.8cm, 2.8cm(L)

p.85 **Pair of Bronze Dou with Handles and Covers**
Eastern Zhou BC 770~221   15cm(H)

p.86 **Archaic Bronze Ding with Cover**
Western Zhou BC 1027~771   21cm(H)

p.87 **Massive size Bronze Steamer**
Spring & Autumn BC 771 - 475   45cm(H)

p.88 **Bronze Hu/Jar with Type 3 Cloud Pattern, Long-Tailed Tadpole Pattern and Tiger Face Handle with Ring**
Spring & Autumn BC 771~475   32cm(H)

p.89 **Bronze Hu/Jar with Chain Handle and Carved Body**
Warring States BC 475~BC 206   40cm(H)

p.90 **Massive Bronze Tripod Vessel with Cover**
Warring States BC 475~BC 206   30cm(H)

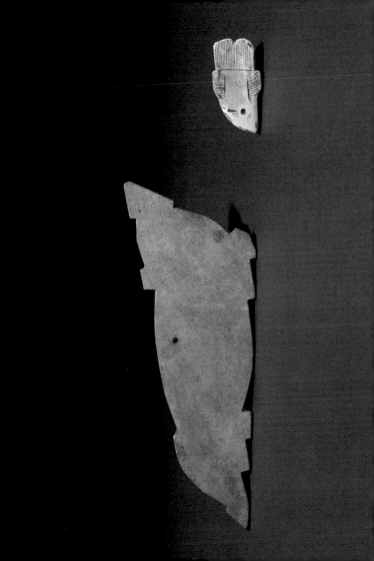

p.92 **Bronze Turquoise, Silver and Gold Inlaid Belt Hook (Dai Gou)**   Warring States BC 475~BC206   17cm(L)

p.93 **Bronze Hu/Jar with Tiger Face Handle and Carved Body with Ring**   Warring States BC 475-221   35cm(H)

p.94 **Bronze Bian Hu, Flattened Jar from Gansu**
Warring States BC 475~BC 206   30cm(H)

p.95 **Bronze Hu/Jar from Gansu**
Warring States BC 475~BC 206   36cm(H)

p.96 **Three Turquoise and Gold Inlaid Belt Hooks (Dai Gou)**
Warring States BC 475~BC 206   10cm(L), 12.5cm(L) , 15cm(L)

p.97 **Bronze Turquoise and Gold Inlaid Belt Hook (Dai Gou)**
Warring States BC 475~BC 206   16cm(L)

p.98 **Gilt Bronze Seal and Silver and Gold Inlaid Staff Finial**
Warring States BC 475~BC 206   5cm, 12 cm(H)

p.100 **Pair of Lead Tiger Weights**
Warring States BC 475-206   5cm(H)

p.101 **Grayish-Olive Glazed Proto-Porcelain Fluted Globular Jar**   Warring States BC 475~BC 206   36.8cm(H)
Oxford TL test no.: p100t81

p.102 **Impressed Grey Pottery Globular Jars**
Warring States BC 475~BC 206   40cm(H), 30cm(H)

p.103 **Rare Painted Grey Pottery Lady with Child**
Warring States BC 475~BC 206   27cm(H)
Oxford TL test no.: c299b75

p.104 **Rare Painted Grey Pottery Lady**
Warring States BC 475~221   30cm(H)
Oxford TL test no.: C199x48

p.105 **Yellow Jade Décor of Sword (Cu Kingdom)**
Warring States BC 475~BC 206   7.8cm(D)

p.106 **Yellow Jade Décor of Sword**
Warring States BC 475~BC 206   3.8cm(L)

HAN BC 206-AD 220

$\mathcal{T}$he first emperor of the Han Dynasty Liu Bong was an officer of the Qin. When he failed to send workmen to build the palace for the emperor due to unfortunate circumstances, he joined a peasant revolt that overthrew the emperor and established the Han dynasty.

Liu Bong located his first capital in Xian in the western part of the empire (Western Han); later this capital was moved to the eastern part of the empire (Eastern Han). The reign of his son and grandson became known as the "Man Jin" period, a time of prosperity and stability.

The Western Han saw a revival of the arts and an intellectual renaissance. Bronze craft, lacquer, jade, painting, and sculpture all reflected the change as demonstrated by the contents of great tombs in Hebei. The intellectual release effected by the removal of Shih Huang Ti's oppression of theoretical discussion and writing led to a burst of creative scholarship. Texts were edited and historical documents scanned to reach an objective level. Also, popular superstition and mythology became respectable among the educated. The stories of mythical emperors and cultural heroes were collected. The cosmology of shamanism was present, with ideas of a

p.108 **Rare finely Modeled Painted Grey Pottery Figure of a Lady**   Western Han BC 206~AD 8   72cm(H)
Oxford TL test no.: c299h61

central heaven supported by a pillar along which spirits could pass between this world and the spirit world. Ideas of this order entered Chinese art, as seen in the cosmic mountain of the incense burner, where there were immortals and cloud scroll décor. During the 2nd century Han art was characterized by realism, which appeared in greater measure in pottery figures of horses and riders found in Shensi.

In Eastern Han art, the bronze works of the traditional kind in massive ornamental vessels or fine inlay of silver and gold were seldom executed. The most notable technical advancement of the Eastern Han period was the development of ceramic glaze. Yet, it was not until the end of the 1st century that a form of green hard glaze was moderately refined. Green and brown glaze was perfected in Henan, Shensi and Shandong, as well as the well-known Yueh ware in Chekiang and Kiangsu. Figures of soldiers, servants, and models of houses, farms, and potters' workshops were placed in tombs perpetuating the objects and scenes of every day life.

p.110 **Painted Grey Earthenware Figure**
Western Han BC 206~AD 8   60 cm(H)
Oxford TL test no.: c299e83

REPRESENTATIVE ILLUSTRATIONS

Western Han BC 206~AD 8   62 cm(H)
Oxford TL test no.: 199y27

p.113 **Grey Earthenware Figure**
Western Han BC 206~AD 8   63 cm(H)
Oxford TL test no.: c100m53

p.114 **Grey Earthenware Figure**
Western Han BC 206~AD 8   63 cm(H)
Oxford TL test no.: c100m53

p.115 **Grey Earthenware Figure**
Western Han BC 206~AD 8   60 cm(H)
Oxford TL test no.: c100m53

p.116 **Grey Earthenware Figure**
Western Han BC 206~AD 8   60 cm(H)
Oxford TL test no.: c199x24

p.117 **Grey Earthenware Figure**
Western Han BC 206~AD 8   60 cm(H)

p.118 **Pair of Painted Grey Pottery Figures of Horses**
Western Han BC 206~AD 8   31cm (H)
Oxford TL test no.: c198s54

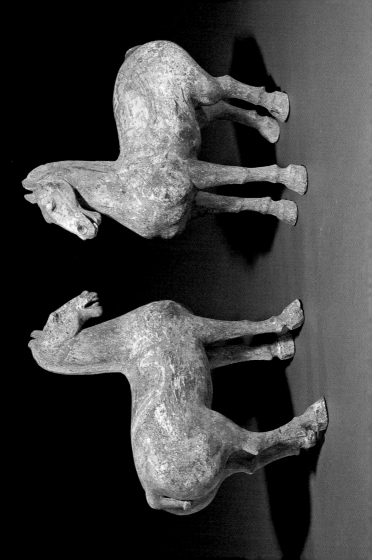

p.120 **Three Painted Grey Pottery Equestrian Figures from Xian**   Western Han BC 206~AD 8   29.2cm (H)
Oxford TL test no. : c198s54

p.121 **Grey Earthenware Horse with Rider**
Western Han BC 206~AD 8   50 cm(H)
Oxford TL test no.: c299629

p.122 **Painted Grey Pottery of a Horse from Shun Tung**
Western Han BC 206~AD 8   29cm(H)

p.123 **Close-up of Item p.121**

p.124 **Yueh Ware Green-glazed Hu/Jar**
Western Han BC 206~AD 8   18cm(H)

p.126 **Large Red Pottery Sichuan Horse**
Eastern Han AD 23~AD 220   105cm(H)
Oxford TL test no.: c199q29

p.127 **Rare Large Sichuan Pottery Figure of a Drummer**
Eastern Han AD 23~AD 220   50cm(H)
HKU TL test no.: 97A13   Similar Sample of Oxford TL test no.: c97e98

p.128 **Large Sichuan Painted Pottery Figure of an Entertainer**
Eastern Han AD 23~AD 220   54cm(H)
Oxford TL test no.: 866f3

p.129 **Large Red Pottery Sichuan Horse**
Eastern Han AD 23~AD 220   50cm(H)

p.130 **The other side of item p.129**

p.131 **Rare Sichuan Pottery Figure of a Foreigner holding a Cross**   Eastern Han AD 23~AD 220   20cm(H)

p.132 **Large Sichuan Pottery Figure of a Witch Doctor**
Eastern Han AD 23~AD 220   105cm(H)
Oxford TL test no.: c299k57

p.134 **Amber-glazed Red Pottery Figure of a Seated Dog**
Eastern Han AD 23~AD 220   30cm(H)
Oxford TL test no.: c199q38

p.135 **Amber-glazed Red Pottery Mask**
Eastern Han AD 23~AD 220   27cm(H)

p.136 **Rare Massive Amber-glazed Red Pottery Figure of a Horse**   Eastern Han AD 23~AD 220   115cm(H)
Oxford TL test no.: c198s91

p.137 **Green-glazed Pottery Incense Burner**
Eastern Han AD 23~AD 220   20cm(H)

p.138 **Two Green-glazed Pottery Figures of Granary**
Eastern Han AD 23~AD 220

p.139 **Green-glazed Pottery Lamp Stand**
Eastern Han AD 23~AD 220   30cm(H)
Oxford TL test no.:

p.140 **Rare Green-glazed Pottery Table with Detachable Legs**
Eastern Han AD 23~AD 220   40cm(L)

p.142 **Two Green-glazed Pottery Figures of Granaries**
Eastern Han AD 23~AD 220   45cm(H)

p.143 **Rare Green-glazed Pottery Hu/Jar**
Eastern Han AD 23~AD 220   40cm(H)

p.144 **Rare Green-glazed Pottery Hu/Jar**
Eastern Han AD 23~AD 220   32cm(H)

p.145 **Green-glazed Pottery Watch Tower with Figures**
Eastern Han AD 23~AD 220   65cm(H)

p.146 **Pair of Green-glazed Pottery Granary Jars**
Eastern Han AD 23~AD 220   27cm(H)

p.147 **Rare Green-glazed Pottery Hu/Jar with Cover**
Eastern Han AD 23~AD 220   38cm(H)

p.148 **Green-glazed Pottery Model of a Pigsty**
Eastern Han AD 23~AD 220   23cm(D)

p.149 **Large Green-glazed Baluster Storage Hu/Jar**
Han BC 206~AD 220   38cm(H)

p.150 **Three Green-glazed Pottery Stoves**
Eastern Han AD 23~AD 220   30cm(L), 32cm(L), 26cm(L)

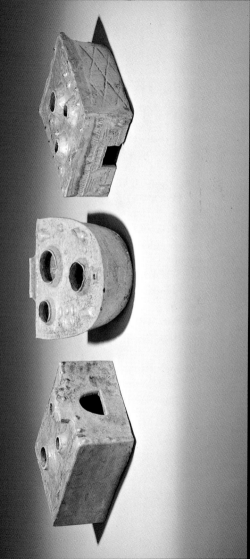

REPRESENTATIVE ILLUSTRATIONS

p.152 **Pair of Green-glazed Prottery Figures of a Duck and a Chicken**   Eastern Han AD 23~AD 220   18cm(H)

p.153 **Green-glazed Pottery Well Head** Han BC 206~AD 220   23cm(H)

p.154 **Yellowish Glazed Lei with Mould-Impressed Décor (Yueh Ware)**   Western Han BC 206~AD 8   32cm(H)

p.155 **Yellowish Glazed Tall-necked Hu with two Loop-Handles (Yueh Ware)**   Western Han BC 206~AD 8   43cm(H)

p.156 **Yellowish Glazed Tall-necked Hu/Jar with two Loop-Handles (Yueh Ware)**   Western Han BC 206~AD 8   45cm(H)

p.157 **Rare Tall-necked Bronze Vase with Chain Décor on the Base**   Western Han BC 206~AD 9   27cm(H)

p.158 **Rare Bronze Hu/Jar with Chain Handles, decorated with Animal Patterns** Western Han BC 206~AD 9   25cm(H)

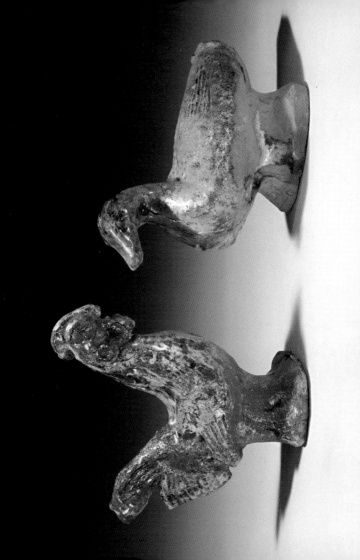

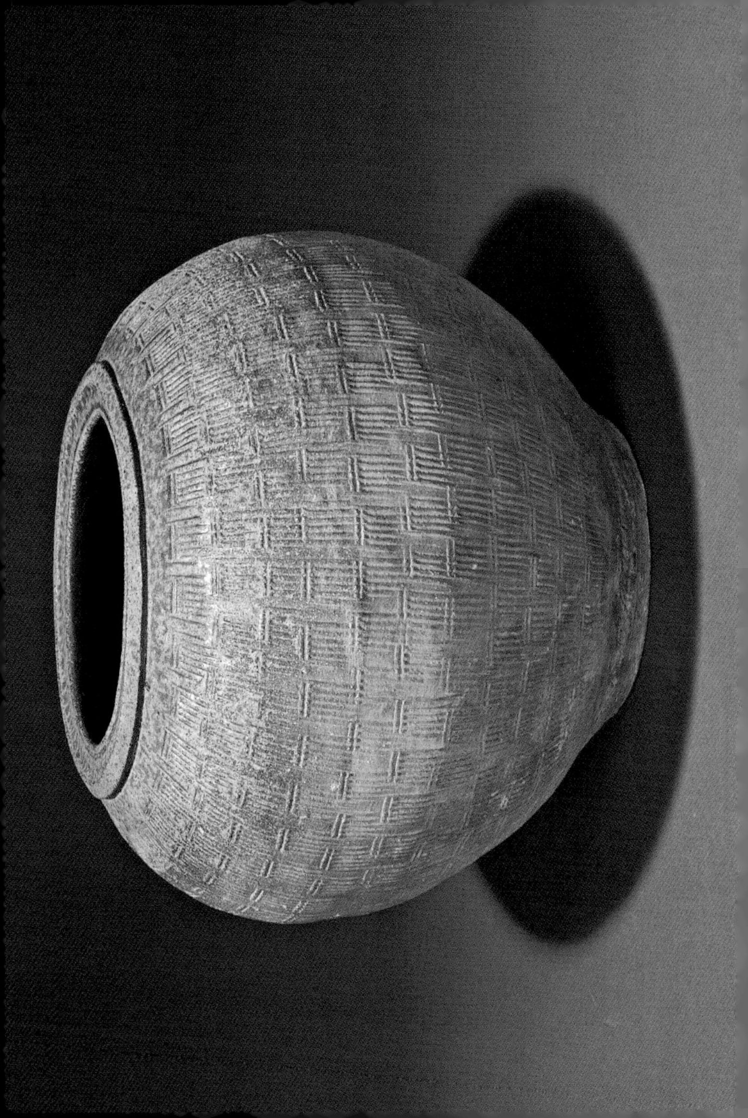

p.160 **Black LacqueredWooden Horse**
Western Han BC 206~AD 9   61cm(H)

p.161 **Green Jade Bi with Dragon Pattern**
Western Han BC 206~AD 9   8.8cm(D)

p.162 **Agate Sword-Scabbord Décoration**
Western Han BC 206~AD 9   5.5cm(L)

THREE KINGDOMS   A.D.220-265

𝒯he collapse of the Eastern Jin Dynasty ushered in a period of over 300 years of disunity, known as the Six Dynasties period, covering the epochs of the Three Kingdoms, Western and Eastern Jin, and Northern and Southern Dynasties. The Han dynasty was weakened by the Yellow Turban uprising, leading to a period of warlords and incessant warfare between the kingdoms of Shu Han, Wei, and Wu. Cao Cao succeeded in wiping out most of the northern warlords, bringing the Yellow River valley under his control. In 220 Cao Pi, Cao Cao's eldest son, overthrew the Han emperor and established the kingdom of Wei, making Luoyand his capital. In 221 Liu Bei proclaimed himself emperor of Shu with Chendu his capital, and in 229 Sun Quan made himself emperor of the Wu with its capital now Nanjing.

p.164 **Four Painted Grey Pottery Figures of Ladies**   20cm(H)
　　　Oxford TL test no.: c299c85

p.165 **Rare Painted Grey Pottery Figure of a Soldier**   35cm(H)
　　　Oxford TL test no.:c199x26

p.166 **Rare Painted Grey Pottery Figure of an Ox and Cart**   60cm(L)

JIN A.D.264-420

$\mathcal{I}$n 263 Wei conquered Shu and two years later Sima Yan forced the Wei emperor to abdicate and he established the Jin Dynasty (Western Jin) with the capitol remaining in Luoyang. In 280 Jin conquered Wu, the last of the Three Kingdoms reuniting the country. The Western Jin allowed peasants to own land, created a system of "nine official grades" and a noble class of princes.

During this extended period painted gray ware figures remained popular in northern China. Nomadic figures from the north also began to emerge, depicting non-Chinese nomads, camels, and beasts with human faces. Green ware broke free from the Han style of replicating bronzes. New shapes included the hun-p'ing, the bear lamp, the tsun jar with mythical beast décor, lion or goat shaped candle holders, the chicken's head ewer, the hu-tzu urine pot, and the kuan jar with lotus décor. Also, the hun-p'ing or spirit jar emerges in this period. This period also saw black glaze at the Te-ching kilns in Chekiang in southern China. Primitive green ware with a black-brown glaze is seen from T'un-his in Anhwei, but this is rare. Archeological evidence shows that contemporary potters understood the importance of iron for determining glaze color.

Buddhist-inspired decorative motifs exerted considerable

p.168 **Painted Grey Pottery Figures of a Horseman and Horse**
   30cm(H)   Oxford TL test no.: c199c12

influence throughout the Eastern Jin (Chin) dynasty. Buddhism pervaded every level of society, as seen in the lotus motif as a dominant feature in both shaping and ornamentation.

Ceramic production at the time centered principally in three great systems, the Yueh ware family of Kiangsu and Chekiang region, the Hungchow ware family of Kiangsi, Hunan, Hupeh, and Szechwan, and the greenishh-brown glaze wares of Fukien and Kwangtung. The Yueh ware produced in this period is highly prized by collectors.

p.170 **Te-Ching Ware Black Glazed Kuan and a Hu with Chicken's Head Décor** 14cm(H), 24cm(H)

p.171 **Sichuan Painted Grey Pottery Figure of a Chimera, Bixie** 48cm(H)
Oford TL test no.: c199w89

p.172 **Two Rare Yueh Ware Green Granary Jars Ku-Tsang Kuan** Jin AD 265~420 44cm(H), 50cm(H)

p.173 **Close up of Item p.174**

p.174 **Rare Yueh Ware Greenish-glazed Kuan with Animal Décor Loop Handles** 18cm(H)

NORTHERN & SOUTHERN DYNASTIES A.D.420-589

Following the death of Sima Yan, internecine war erupted known as the "Disturbances of the Eight Princes" The short-lived Western Jin period ended in 316. This was followed by a period known as the Northern and Southern Dynasties, when China was divided with the North eventually ruled by T'o-pa Tartars, and the South by Chinese (Northern and Southern Dynasties, 420-589).

From the late Han period through the Jin period, conflict with Mongolian tribes grew fiercer. In BC 200 the first Han emperor, Liu Bong, led his 300,000 strong army to fight against the Mongolians at Shanxi, Tai Yuen. He lost the battle and had to pay tribute to escape. Between BC 200-134 seven princesses were sent to marry Mongolian tribesmen to maintain peace. Finally in AD 439 Tuobadao, emperor of the Northern Wei unified Northern China under his rule. This was the beginning of the Northern Dynasty and marked the first time the Mongolians took over China.

In these confusing times, the country became sharply divided. In AD 543 Prime Minister of the Northern Wei, Gao Huan, established the Eastern Wei (AD 534-550) at Luoyang, while another general, Yu Wen Tai established the Western Wei (AD 535-556) at Xian. Finally in AD 549 Gao Yang conquered the Eastern

p.176 **Rare Wooden Figure of a Camel**
Northern & Southern Dynasties AD 386~589   50cm(H)

Wei and formed the Northern Qi (AD549-577), as a Mongolian state. Meanwhile, Yu Wen Jue took over the Western Wei to establish the Northern Zhou (AD557-581), following the Han manner of rule.

The country was only unified under the Sui dynasty under Emperor Sui Wen in AD 581.

p.178 **Painted Grey Pottery Figure of a Horse**
     Northern Wei AD 386~535   29cm(H)
     Oxford TL test no.: c100t84

p.179 **Pair of Painted Grey Pottery Figures of a Couples**
     Early Northern Wei AD 386~535   30cm(H)

p.180 **Rare Painted Grey Pottery Figure of Horse in Full Amour**   Northern Wei AD386~535   37.5cm(H)
     Oxford TL test no.: c298h21

p.181 **Close up of Item p.182**

p.182 **Rare Painted Grey Pottery Figure of a Caparisoned Horse**   Northern Wei AD 386~535   35cm(H)
     Oxford TL test no.: c299d74

p.184 **Three Painted Grey Pottery Ladies**
Northern Wei AD 386~535   31cm(H)

p.185 **Four Painted Grey Pottery Soldiers**
Northern Qi AD 550~577   30cm(H)

p.186 **Three Painted Grey Pottery Horses with Riders**
Northern Qi AD 550~577   33cm(H)
Oxford TL test no.: c199q43

p.187 **Rare Pair of Painted Grey Pottery Soldiers**
Northern Qi AD 550~577   40cm(H)

p.188 **Rare Pair of Painted Grey Pottery Camels**
Northern Zhou AD 557~581   23cm(H)

p.190 **Yueh Ware Greenish Glazed Ewer**
Southern Dynasty AD420~589   23cm(H)

p.191 **Stone Head of a Guardian**
Northern & Southern Dynasties AD 386~589   23cm(H)

p.192 **Rare Stone Head of Buddha**
Northern & Southern Dynasties AD 386~589   30cm(H)

SUI A.D.589-618

The Chinese Empire was reunited after eight years of civil war under Yan Chien, the founder of the Sui dynasty in AD589. Yan Chien proved to be a highly capable emperor. He was humble and honest, thereby his reign became associated with the "Man Jin" period of the early Han. His reign allowed prosperity, which would be reflected in the beauty of its arts. His son proved to be corrupt, inefficient, and self-indulgent. The Sui dynasty only lasted three decades before being eclipsed by the Tang dynasty. Thus the Sui dynasty should be seen as a transition between the Southern and Northern Dynasties and the Tang dynasty.

The popularity of the acanthus leaf motif in the Sui period meant that the original lotus pattern was gradually superseded by patterns of geometrically arranged acanthus leaves.

Moreover, the majority of ceramic wares popular during the Tang, with the exceptional of three-color ware and decorate ware, emerged in the Sui period. This makes it difficult to distinguish Sui and Tang ceramics. Still certain characteristics are unique to Sui ceramics. Sui dynasty flasks always have moulded decoration while the flat dishes normally have a carved decoration. Also, applied application was less evident in the Sui period. While Central

p.194 **Painted Sandstone Head of GuanYin**   25cm(H)

Asian influences were evident in both Sui and Tang dynasties, grape flowers and Central Asian dancers and musicians mostly occur on Sui pieces. Certain subtle stylistic changes can be seen between Sui and Tang ceramics. Sui ceramics tend to consist of gray or red painted ware, while Tang included red and white painted ware, as well as three-color wares. Tang figures appear livelier, with articulated joints to provide movement.

p.196 **Pair of Yellowish Glazed White Pottery Horses**
30cm(H)   Similar Sample of Oxford TL test no.: c97q45

p.197 **Yueh Ware Greenish-Glazed Pear Shaped Vase**   32cm(H)

p.198 **Yellowish Glazed White Pottery Figure of a Horse and a Female Dancer**   30cm(H)
Oxford TL test no.: c199f98

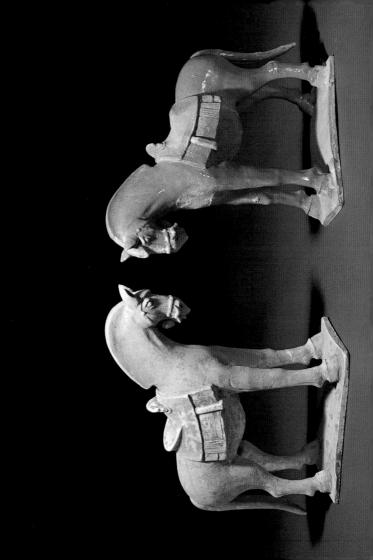

TANG A.D.618-907

Considered the Golden Age in Chinese history, the Tang Dynasty spanned nearly 300 years from the early 7th century to 10th century. There were great advances made in the sciences, medicine and technology; woodblock printing and gunpowder were invented. A strong central government brought about a period of great economic and cultural prosperity. The boundaries of the empire continued to expand to Central Asia in the west, Korea in the East, and Vietnam in the South.

Tang emperors were patrons of art and sponsors of massive building projects. For instance, the 2nd emperor, Tang Taizong was a poet as well as a calligrapher. Tang Ming Huang (Xuanzong) was a calligrapher and a musician.

Tang was well known for its Sancai polychrome pottery. Sancai refers to three colors namely yellow, green and brown. The best knowns are the horse figures. Horses were admired because of their speed and endurance, and were indispensable in warfare, hunting and the aristocratic pastime of polo playing. Camel figures were also important, as camels were crucial in trade and cultural exchange between China and the Middle East through the famous Silk Road. They represented the continuance of prosperity and wealth. Some camel

p.200 **Rare Painted Grey Pottery Figure of a Camel**
Early Tang   40cm(H)
HKU TL test no.: 97A36

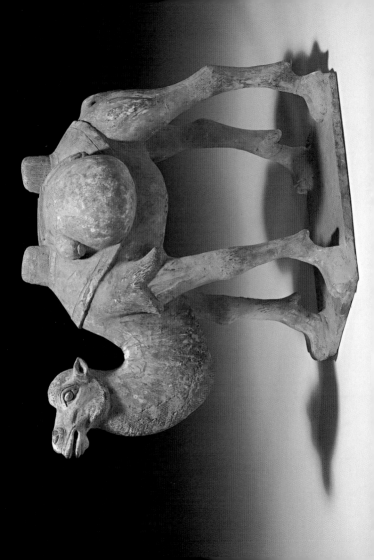

figures have saddlebags with a guardian monster mask.

Early Tang figures are always stiff and in columnar form with the limbs close to the body. The Hu people were a popular theme and were usually depicted as bearded and half-naked. The tomb guardian, called Tian Wang, was protector of the four cardinal directions. Later in the Tang dynasty, figures have striking sculptural quality. For this reason, Tang Pottery can be found in many of the world's museums for their unsurpassed level of artistry.

p.202 **Rare Painted Grey Pottery Group of a Horse and Rider**
Early Tang   48cm (H)
Oxford TL test no.: c97c40

p.203 **Rare Painted Grey Pottery Group of a Horse and Rider**
Early Tang   40cm (H)
Oxford TL test no.: c97a77

p.204 **Rare Painted Grey Pottery Group of a Horse and Rider**
Early Tang   41.9cm (H)
Oxford TL test no. :c97d23

p.206 **Rare Painted Pottery Figure of a Lokapala**
Tang AD 618~907   45cm(H)

p.207 **Rare Painted Pottery Figure of a Lokapala**
Tang AD618~907   50cm(H)

p.208 **Rare Painted Red Pottery Figure of an Earth Spirit on a Wild Pig**   Tang AD618~907   50cm(H)
Oxford TL test no.: c100t80

p.209 **Painted Red Pottery Figure of a Foreigner**
Tang AD 618~907   45cm(H)

p.210 **Painted Pottery Court Lady**
Tang AD 618~907   38cm(H)

p.211 **Painted Pottery Figure of an Earth Spirit**
Tang AD 618~907   45cm(H)
Oxford TL test no.: c101e44

p.212 **Pair of Well Modeled Painted Pottery Court Ladies**
Tang AD618~907   40cm(H)
Oxford TL test no.: c100d72, c100b42

p.213 **Painted Well Modeled Pottery Figure of a Court Lady**
Tang AD 618~907   37cm(H)
Oxford TL test no.: c100g71

p.214 **Pair of Painted Pottery Court Ladies**
Tang AD 618~907
Oxford TL test no.: c100m16, c100e81

p.216 **Painted Red Pottery Figure of a Horse**
Tang AD618~907   50cm(H)
Oxford TL test no.: c299k20

p.217 **Painted White Pottery Figure of a Prancing Horse**
Tang AD 618~907   53cm(H)
Oxford TL test no.: c199u2

p.218 **Painted White Pottery Figure of a Prancing Horse**
Tang AD 618~907   45cm(H)
Oxford TL test no.: c199j99

p.219 **Large Painted Pottery Figure of a Standing Camel**
Tang AD 618~907   45cm(H)
Oxford TL test no.: c199y18

p.220 **Rare Pair of Painted White Pottery Figures of Polo-players**   Tang AD 618~907   27cm(H)
Oxford TL test no.: C100s85, c100s83

p.221 **Pair of Painted Grey Pottery Figures of Horses and Riders**   Tang AD 618-907   35cm(H)
Oxford TL test no.: c199jp8

p.222 **Rare Pair of Painted White Pottery Figures of Horses with Lady Riders**   40cm(H)
HKU TL test no.: 9784

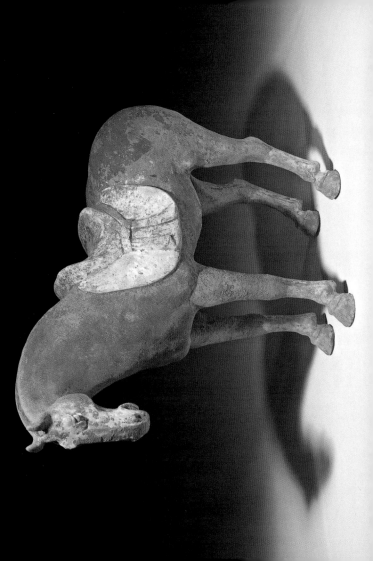

p.224 **Rare Sancai Glazed Pottery Dish with Cobalt Blue**
Tang AD 618-907   14cm(D)

p.225 **Rare Sancai Glazed Pottery Figure of a Horse and Rider with Cobalt Blue**   Tang AD 618~907   45cm(H)
Oxford TL test no.: c100u41

p.226 **Rare Sancai Glazed Figure of a Camel with Cobalt Blue**
Tang AD 618~907   35cm(H)
Oxford TL test.: c100d64

p.227 **Sancai Glazed Figure of an Earth Spirit with Cobalt Blue**
Tang AD 618~907   40cm(H)

p.228 **Rare Sancai Glazed Figure of a seated Court Lady with Cobalt Blue**   Tang AD 618-907   30cm(H)
Oxford TL test no.: 866e93

p.230 **Sancai Glazed Figure of a Civil Officer**
Tang AD 618~907   76cm(H)

p.231 **Close up of item p.230**

p.232 **Rare, Well-modeled Sancai Glazed Pottery Figure of a Horse**   Tang AD 618-907   50cm(H)
Oxford TL test no.: c97v47

p.233 **Chang Sha Porcelain Dish**
Tang AD618~907   6.5cm(D)

p.234 **Three Chang Sha Miniature Figures**
Tang AD618~907   5cm(H), 5.5cm(H), 17cm(H)

REPRESENTATIVE ILLUSTRATIONS

p.236 **Limestone Head of Buddha**
Tang AD 618~907　8cm(H)

p.237 **Sandstone Head of Buddha**
Tang AD 618~907　20cm(H)

p.238 **Sandstone Head of Buddha**
Tang AD 618~907　23cm(H)

p.239 **White Jade Buckle**
Tang AD618~907　3.5cm(H)

p.240 **White Jade Ram**
Tang AD 618~907　4.5cm(H)

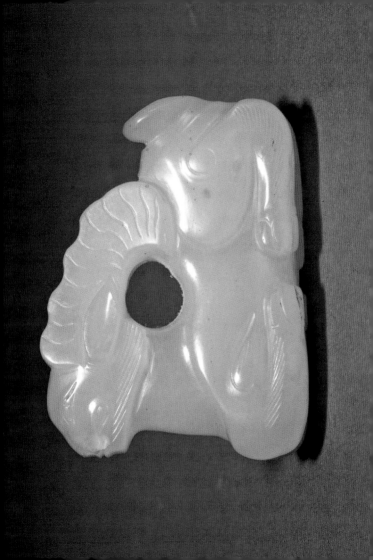

SONG A.D.960-1279

$\mathcal{T}$he Song Dynasty was founded in AD 960 and lasted until 1279. It was a dynasty with periods of brilliance and local prosperity, but the whole of China was never under a firm rule during the Song Dynasty. Its capital was in the valley of the Huang He (Yellow River). In 1127 the capital had to be withdrawn first to Naking and then to Hangchow in the lower Yangtze valley. During this period, the Song Dynasty slowly lost its fight with invaders. One of them was the Liao tribe, a nomadic people of partly Turkish, partly Mongol origins. By the beginning of 12th century they ruled all North China down to the Yellow River, with its capital at Peking. Instead of conquering the Song, however, the Liao demanded large indemnities and tributes in silk and money. In spite of their military weakness the Sung Dynasty kept up a high and even luxurious culture in terms of art, literature and philosophy.

Early Song rulers emphasized centralization of power and administration in order to prevent the rise of regional warlords. The opening of the Grand Canal linking north and south, and the expansion of trade with Inner Asia all stimulated the economy. From the late Tang and continuing throughout the Song, commerce flourished at all levels. Due to the concentration of people and wealth

p.242 **Painted Stucco Head of Buddha**   46cm(H)

in great cities, a distinctly urban style of life evolved. Entertainment quarters emerged. Apart form that, luxury goods available in the great cities reached artistic levels rarely surpassed. The Song Dynasty was the Golden Age of Chinese Ceramics. The exuberant beauty of the Ru, Guan, Ge, Ding, Jun, Celadon, Yaozhou, Ding, Cizhou, Raozhou, Yingqing and Jizhou wares has won numerous commendations.

p.244 **Three Stucco Figures of Celestial Officers**   37cm(H)

REPRESENTATIVE ILLUSTRATIONS

p.246 **Pair of Sandstone Lions**   40cm(H)

p.247 **Painted Sandstone Head of Buddha**   25cm(H)

p.248 **Painted Sandstone Head of a Buddha**   29cm(H)

p.249 **Ying Qing Covered Ewer**   16cm(H)

p.250 **Pair of Massive Ying Qing Funerary Vases with Covers**
80cm(H)

p.251 **Ying Qing Covered Ewer**   8.5cm(H)

p.252 **Ying Qing Cosmetics Box and a Waterdropper in the
shape of a Lion**   8cm(D), 6cm(L)

p.253 **Brown Glazed Ewer with Overhead Handle (Cizhou
Ware)**   19cm(H)

p.254 **Green Glazed Yaozhou Ware Tiger**   7cm(L)

p.255 **Basin with Handle Decorated with Moulded Pattern
under Greyish Green Glaze (Guan Ware)**   9.8cm(D)

p.256 **White Jade Pi Xie Buckle**   6cm(L)

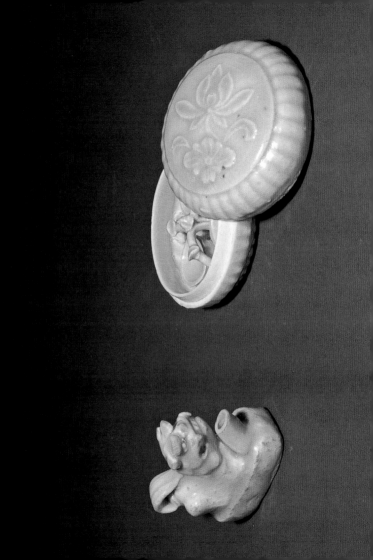

YUAN A.D.1271-1368

$\mathcal{T}$he Mongols were the first inner Asian nomadic people to conquer and rule all of China. When the Mongols under Genghis Khan conquered China in 1210, the warring states were brought under one rule. Several Mongol empires were formed after the death of Genghis Khan in Central Asia, southern Russia, and Persia. In China, the Yuan dynasty was established 1271 A.D. with the capital in Peking. While the Mongols in Mongolia distrusted the distant emperor in China, who was no longer a nomadic warrior and seemed to be more Chinese, the Chinese resented these invaders. Peasant revolts in the Yangtze valley, weakened the power of the state. Out of the fighting, Zhu Yuan Zhang, a lowly peasant, overthrew the Mongolian invaders and founded the Ming Dynasty in the Middle of the 14th century.

Regarding culture and art, the Mongols had a zest for the theater, music and traditional Chinese theatrical opera. In the arts, the most important innovation came with the development of under-glaze blue and red ware. Under-glaze blue ceramics were made by using cobalt paint on the body before coating the entire vessel in a transparent glaze and firing. Red under-glaze was achieved by using copper as the pigment.

p.258 **Two Limestone Panels from Temple**   55cm(H)

p.260 **Ying Qing Horse and Dog** 14cm(H), 11cm(H)
Chinese University TL test no.: 02183

p.261 **Set of Four Black Pottery Horses and Figures** 30cm(H)
Oxford TL test no.: c199e14

p.262 **Set of Three Painted Horses with Riders** 35cm(H)
Oxford TL test.: c199j76

p.263 **Lamp Stand with Celadon Glaze** 18cm(H)

p.264 **Small Junyao Bowl** 11cm(D)

p.265 **White Jade Waterpot with Black Mottles** 5.8cm(L)

p.266 **White Jade Flower with Brown Markings** 6.2cm(H)

MING A.D.1368-1644

The founder of the Ming Dynasty, Zhu YuanZhang, was a Buddhist priest before joining an anti-Mongol sect known as the Red Turbans. He eventually achieved supreme power within the rebel movement and overthrew the Yuan Dynasty, becoming the Emperor Hongwu. Zhu Yuanzhang's son, who reigned as the Yongle Emperor, continued the aggressive, despotic policies of his father. He led various military expeditions against the Mongol tribes. For the sake of peace, Yongle moved the Ming government from Nanjing (south) to Beijing (north). It was in Beijing where he built the huge and impressive palace complex - the Forbidden City.

During the Hongwu period, one saw the production of fine under-glaze red ware, while under-glaze blue ware from the Yongle period was well known for a clear body and glaze as well as a strong blue color. Over-glaze decoration also underwent a dramatic development. Wucai, literally "five-color" enamelware from the Jiajing and Wanli periods was bright and colorful. The Yixing kilns in Jiangsu province also produced pottery in various colors from light yellow, through reddish brown and purplish black to green.

p.268 **Sandstone Figure of Seated QuanYin**   120cm(H)

p.270 **Painted Stucco Figure of a Seated God of Fortune**
35cm(H)

p.271 **Painted Stucco Figure**   100cm(H)

p.272 **Painted Stucco Figure**   100cm(H)

p.274 **Glazed Green and Orange Horse Figure**
Ming AD 1368~1644   29cm(H)

p.275 **Pair of Blue-Glazed Pottery Figures of a Couple**
Ming AD1368~1644   42cm(H)

p.276 **White Jade Horse and Horseman**
Ming AD1368~1644   15cm(H)

p.277 **Fine and Rare Carved Tianhuang Seal**
17th Century   5cm(H), 71.5gm

p.278 **Gilt Bronze Seated Figure of the Bodhisattva Padmapani**
Ming AD 1368~1644   20cm(H)

p.279 **Blue and White Washer**
Ming AD1368~1644   13cm(D)

p.280 **Junyao Washer**
Ming AD1368~1644   5cm(D)

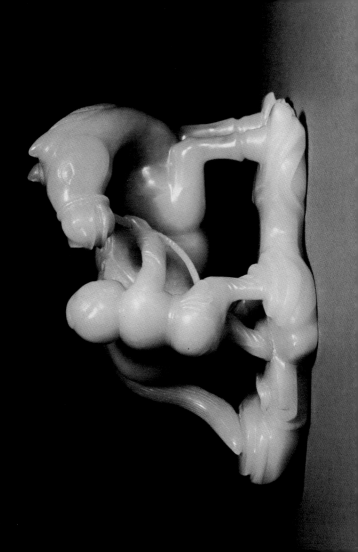

QING A.D.1644-1911

$\mathcal{W}$eak and self-indulgent emperors, official corruption, bureaucratic factionalism and abuse of power characterized the late Ming Dynasty. Together with the neglect of public works by the court and natural disaster, this gave rise to rebellion. In the northeastern area of Liandong, a tribal confederation known as the Manchus joined the Ming troops under Wu Sangui to expel the rebels. The Manchus then dedlared that they had saved China and founded the Qing dynasty in 1644 AD.

The later decline of the Qing dynasty involved internal and external problems. Domestically, population increased dramatically and created a lot of social problems. During the 19th century, various incidents made people see that changes were needed to save China; the opium war (1839-42) led to a series of unequal treaties, the presence of Empress Cixi (1835-1908) who manipulated the succession law & the Sino-Japanese war (1894-95). Dr. Sun Zhongshan (1866-1925) was among the western-educated individuals who believed China's salvation could only be found in revolution. In 1911-1912, the republican revolutionaries under Sun Zhongshan overthrew imperial power.

While the Qing period is seen historically as a period of

p.282 **Pair of Incised Blue Back Dishes Seal, Mark and Period of Yongzheng** 18.8cm(D)

decline, culture flourished. Many innovations were made during the reigns of the Emperors Kangxi, Yongzheng and Qianlong. New types of glaze color included peach blossom, sky blue, ocean blue, imperial yellow, and others. Ceramic production reached a zenith in the Qianlong period. There was a large variety of glaze colors, while shapes and forms often embodied auspicious meanings. Apart from that Qing scholars wrote a number of excellent works of fiction, including the masterpiece "Dream of the Red Chamber" by Cao Xueqin.

p.284 **Celadon Glazed Jar, Seal Mark and Period of Yongzheng** 21.5cm(H)

p.286 **Fine Pair Blue and White Lingzhi Bowls, Seal Marks and Period of Qianlong**   11.5cm(D)

p.287 **Fine Blue and White Stemcup, Seal Mark and Period of Daoguang**   8.5m(H)

p.288 **Fine Pair of Blue and White Yuhu Chun Ping Seal, Mark and Period of Daoguang**   28cm(H)

p.289 **Celadon Glazed Cong-Shaped Vase, Seal Mark and Period of Guangxu**   28cm(H)

p.290 **Unusual Guan-Type Tree Trunk-Shaped Brush Pot**
18th Century   11cm(H)

p.291 **Finely Cast Gilt-Bronze Figure of the Lama Zong KaBa**
18th Century   18cm(H)

p.292 **Pair of Rare and Fine Gilt Wood GuanYins Holding Children**   18th Century   16cm(H)

p.293 **Rare and Fine Carved TianHuang Seal**
18th Century   4.8cm(H), 36 gm

p.294 **Fine and Carved "Brown Furong" Seal**
18th Century   3cm(H)

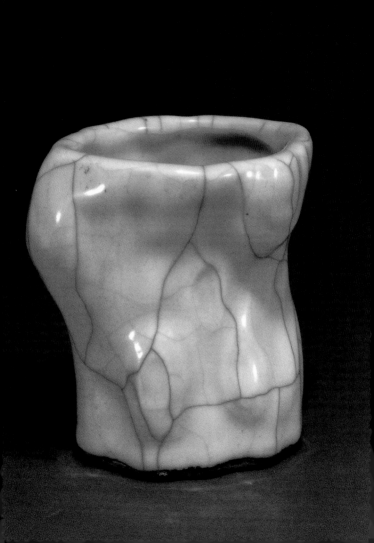

REPRESENTATIVE ILLUSTRATIONS

p.296 **Yi Xing Fruits by Chen Ming Yuan with Seal Marks**
18th Century 3.5cm(D), 7.8cm(L), 3.3cm(L), 3cm (L)

p.297 **White Beijing Glass Snuff Bottle with Red-Overlay**
18th Century 6.3cm(H)

p.298 **Brown Beijing Glass Snuff Bottle with Blue-Overlay**
19th Century 5.5cm(H)

p.299 **Black and White Suzhou Jade Snuff Bottle**
18th Century 8.5cm(H)

p.300 **Opposite side of item p.299**

p.301 **White Jade Two-Part Belt Buckle**
18th Century 11cm(L)

p.302 **Three White Jade Carvings**
6.2cm(L) 8cm(L), 7.cm(L)

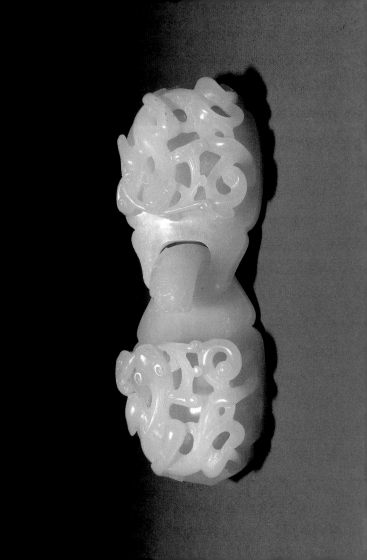

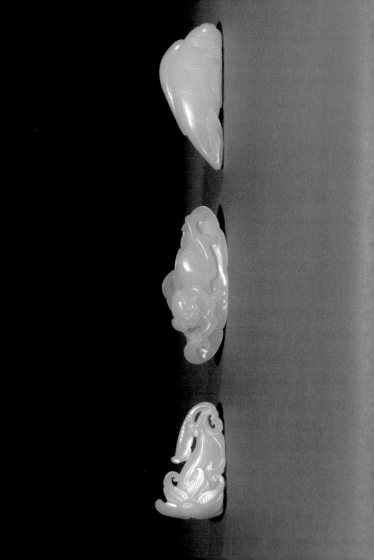

EARLY 20TH CENTURY

Jindezhen has been the centre for the manufacture of porcelain since the Yuen dynasty (A.D.1279-1368) and imperial kilns were set up during the Ming and Qing dynasties.

In the late Qing, semi-governmental porcelain companies were established against competition from Japan and the west and even imperial pieces were contracted out to commercial kilns. With the demise of Qing in 1911, the imperial factory was closed down and all the craftsmen were disposed of. These craftsmen established their own workshops and gained creative freedom.

A traditional type of porcelain painting named Qianjang became popular in the late Qing. Qianjiang is a Chinese painting technique used in porcelain, and the outstanding painters of Qianjiang in this period were Pan Taoyu and Wang Xiaotang. Later, imported painting materials were used and made paintings and porcelain paintings even more popular.

Eight painters named Wang Qi, Wang Dafan, Deng Bishan, Xu Zhongnan, Wang Yeting, Tian Hexian, Cheung Yiting and Liu Yucen formed the Yueyuan Hui and people called them the eight friends of Zhushan. Collectors do not have to collect based on the popularity of the artist; the quality of painting on the porcelain is more important.

p.304 **Fine Pair of Blue and White Dragon Pattern Flower Pots**
Early 20th Century   16cm(H)

Schushan, a small village, 100km from the city of Fuzhou is famous for thier mountains of different kinds of soapstone. Artists take advantage of inclusions (natural color of the stone) in their carvings and design composition. The most famous and unusual ones are Tai Huang, Fu Rong, Chi Jiang, Sin Pa Tung, Lichi and Ox-Horn.

p.306 **Unusual "Qianjian" Famille-Rose Panel by Qing Men** 38cm(H)

p.307 **Pair of "European Subject" Famille Rose Vases** 9cm(H)

p.308 **Rare and Fine Carved "Sin Pa Jung" Soap Stone Figure of "Three Drunk Gods" by Zhou Zha Ban** 20cm(L)

p309 **Rare and Fine Carved "Ox-horn Dung" Soap Stone Figure of a Unicorn by Zhou Bo Ting** 9cm(L)

p.310 **Rare and Fine Carved "Chi Jiang" Soap Stone Figure of Tieh Kuai Li by Lin Fa Shu** 31cm(L)

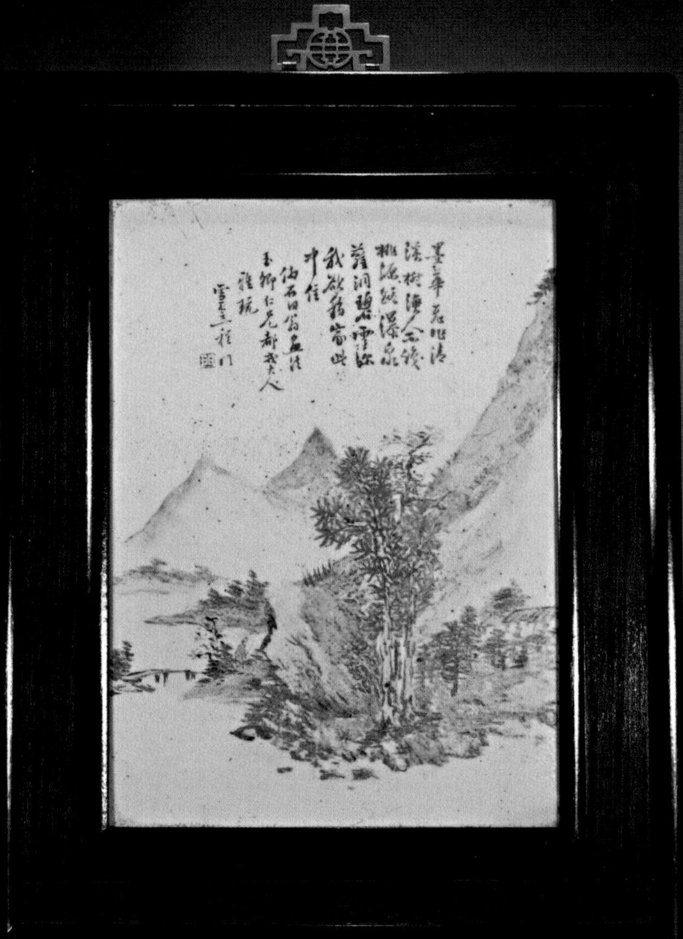
仿石田翁畫法
玉卿仁兄都戎大人
雅玩

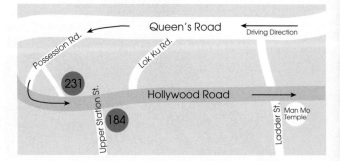

Collecting Chinese Antiquities in Hong Kong

Published by: Dragon Cultrure Ltd.
             184 & 231 Hollywood Road, Hong Kong
             tel: 2545 8098   fax: 2541 1488
             web site: www.dragonculture.com.hk

Editor / Writer: Victor Choi, Ada Yung
Photography: C. L. Chow
Design: Cindy Au Yeung
Printed by: Paramount Printing Company Ltd.